MUSICIANS INSTITUTE

PRIVATE LESSONS

CHART READING WORKBOOK
for drummers

by Bobby Gabriele

Edited by Rick Mattingly

PLAYBACK➕
Speed • Pitch • Balance • Loop

To access audio visit:
www.halleonard.com/mylibrary

Enter Code
6982-8411-0718-6631

ISBN 978-0-7935-7126-0

Visit Hal Leonard Online at
www.halleonard.com

Contact us:
Hal Leonard
7777 West Bluemound Road
Milwaukee, WI 53213
Email: info@halleonard.com

In Europe, contact:
Hal Leonard Europe Limited
42 Wigmore Street
Marylebone, London, W1U 2RN
Email: info@halleonardeurope.com

In Australia, contact:
Hal Leonard Australia Pty. Ltd.
4 Lentara Court
Cheltenham, Victoria, 3192 Australia
Email: info@halleonard.com.au

Acknowledgments

My sincere thanks to:

My parents, for everything;

My brother John, who kindled the spark to write this book;

Joe Porcaro, Ralph Humphrey, and Steve Houghton, who opened my eyes to drumming;

The staff and students of PIT, for their help and feedback in the writing of this book;

Inon Zur (the King of the Keyboards!) for the great musical performances, creativity, friendship and strong coffee;

Dale Adams and Mark Kaufman at Shoelace Studios;

Brent and the folks at Zildjian West for the great sounds;

Jay Morreale at Mystique triggers for his excellent gadgetry;

Rick Mattingly for his expertise editing this project (and answering a lot of dumb questions);

the staff at Hal Leonard, for their insights which allowed me to engrave and layout this book;

And to Kelly.

Notation Key

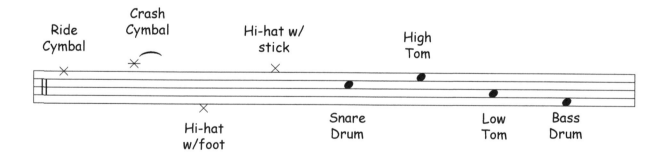

Contents

About The Author

A native of Detroit, Michigan, Bobby Gabriele has been playing drums for more than twenty-five years. He studied percussion and music education at the Interlochen Arts Academy and the University of Michigan, and graduated from the Percussion Institute of Technology (PIT), a division of Musicians Institute (MI), where he was presented with the PIT Humanitarian Of The Year award and a Zildjian endorsement.

Bobby's talents were first noted worldwide with the group Alliance on CBS/ Handshake records. In 1991, his band, The Neutrinos was voted one of LA's top new groups by KLOS.

Since his move to Los Angeles, Bobby has written and/or performed in music for film and TV, including *Beverly Hills 90210*, *Lois And Clark*, *Murder She Wrote*, and the hit movie *Men At Work*. Bobby is currently the drummer for the Alabama Theatre in Myrtle Beach, SC and maintains a busy teaching, performing and recording schedule.

Introduction

There is nothing mystical (or inherently evil) about chart reading.

Simply put, **a chart is the fastest way for the composer to convey musical ideas to the band.** There is no substitute for a musician's ears in the finished product, but by reading the chart and following the composer's ideas, we can save a lot of rehearsal time.

Drumset chart reading can be broken down into three distinct categories: the "groove," or the patterns that are played to establish the time; the "road map," or overall form of the music on the page; and the "figures," which are rhythmic sketches indicating important musical accents.

In simple terms, the drummer's job is to:

- Keep time

- Follow the chart

- Support the figures

In this book, I break down these fundamental concepts and reinforce them with comprehensive, easy-to-follow charts. Using this approach, you can zero in on your difficulties, making you a confident reader and a solid player.

The key to chart reading is repetition of the basics. You will most likely find yourself memorizing certain figures; this is a **good** thing. This is an essential process in building a repertoire of figures and ideas. These ideas are your vocabulary; they are the tools you need to read **any** chart.

This book is written in a swing or big band style; however, these concepts apply to all styles and should be practiced that way.

So don't be intimidated by all those dots on the page. Use them to help you become a better drummer!

Bobby Gabriele

The Road Map I

First of all, let's break down a few of the most common symbols and musical shorthand that are used in chart reading. Once you understand the road map, it's a lot easier to focus on the other elements of the chart.

1. Time Slashes

Instead of writing rhythmic patterns in every measure, copyists often use slashes to indicate time, continuing the groove that has been previously established. Each slash represents one beat in the current time signature. It is common to write measure numbers on top of each bar to remind you how many measures you have played.

2. Measure Repeat Sign

This is musical shorthand to repeat what you played in the previous measure. Again, it is common to write measure numbers on top to remind you how many measures you have repeated.

3. Double Bar

The double bar is used to show the end of a musical phrase. Understanding where phrases occur is essential in chart reading, as these phrase points are often punctuated by fills leading into the next section.

4. Rehearsal Letters

These markers are used to indicate the beginnings of phrases, and they speed up rehearsals by giving the band points of reference. Sometimes letters are used, sometimes numbers, sometimes measure numbers; their purpose is the same.

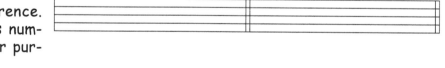

5. Section Repeat Signs

The thick double barlines with the dots facing inward are section repeat signs. When placed around a phrase, the measures between the repeat signs are played again. In this example, you would play from measures 1 through 5, then return to measure 2 and play through bar 5 one more time. Then continue on with the chart (bar 10, etc.).

6. Multiple Section Repeats

When a phrase is repeated several times, it is common to use standard repeat signs and to write the number of total times the section is played. (The notation "X's" is standard shorthand for "times.") In this case, you would play this phrase a total of four times before going on.

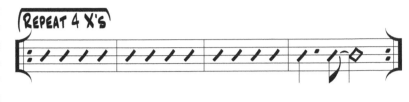

7. Fills and Set-Ups

A *fill* is a drum lead-in into a musical phrase. When a fill leads into a specific rhythmic figure played by the band, it is called a *set-up*. The specific notes of a fill or set-up are rarely written out; it is up to the drummer to decide what to play.

8. Slash Notation

Rhythmic figures supported by the ensemble are "sketched out" using slash noteheads. This technique illustrates the rhythm to be played without dictating the exact orchestration; this allows the players freedom to create their own parts within the structure of the arrangement and saves copyists a lot of time. (Half-note and whole-note heads are written as diamonds.)

9. Fermata or Bird's Eye or Hold

A note or a rest under the fermata is sustained and time is suspended until the conductor or bandleader directs the end of the event. That ending is called a *cut-off*.

10. 8 Bars X, 16 More

Instead of writing each individual measure separately, or writing time slashes or measure repeats indicating a repeated groove, a common musical shorthand is to combine the phrase into one numbered group. Here, you would play eight measures of time, then sixteen more bars of time.

11. First and Second Endings

The brackets above measures 5–6 and 11–12 are first and second ending markings. The first time through measures 1–4, continue through measures 5 and 6 (the first ending); then take the repeat back to measure 1. Then, after playing bars 1–4 the second time, skip over the first ending and go directly to bars 11 and 12 (the second ending).

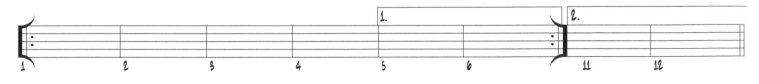

Section Or Ensemble Figures?

Now that you understand the basics of the road map, let's look at the other important part of chart reading: the figures. Written figures in a chart fall into two categories: the *section figure*, and the *ensemble figure*.

*   A *Section Figure* is a musical phrase or accent played by a single section of the band (i.e., trumpets, saxes, trombones, etc.).

*   An *Ensemble Figure* is a phrase or accent played by the entire band.

Distinguishing between the two on the page is easy.

Section Figure

In the above example, time slashes are written in the first two bars, indicating a groove is played. Bars 3 and 4, however, have a rhythm written over them. You can tell this is a section figure by three important distinctions:

*   The rhythm is written **above** the staff.

*   The instruction *trmbn.* indicates which section of the band will play this rhythm.

*   The time slashes continue through the figures.

Ensemble Figure

This example begins the same way as the previous example, but the figures in measures 3 and 4 are different.

*   The notes are written **on** the staff, not above it, replacing the time slashes.

*   The abbreviation *Ens.* indicates that the entire ensemble will play the rhythm.

*   The noteheads are written as slashes, indicating an ensemble approach.

Now that you've identified the different figures on the page, you must understand the differences in terms of your drumming.

Section Figures

With section figures, the role of the drummer is to continue the time and support the figure. You don't want to play too much or too loud, because you might overpower the section of the band you were meant to accompany.

For section figures, the role of the drummer is to:

- Keep the groove going
- Play the figures on snare drum or bass drum

IMPORTANT! When performing section figures, don't play fills or cymbal crashes that would over-emphasize the importance of the figures (as well as drown out the band).

Ensemble Figures

Ensemble figures are a different story. Your role changes to adapt to the importance of the figure, which is being played by the entire band. Now you must temporarily stop the ride cymbal pattern to play a set-up or fill leading into the ensemble figure. Then support the rhythms, crashing cymbals on the important notes.

These are the three keys to playing ensemble figures:

- Stop playing the ride pattern (as necessary)
- Play a set-up leading into the figure
- Play the figure, crashing cymbals on the important notes

Train Wrecks

In my experience, the major "train wrecks" in chart reading occur not in the timekeeping part of the chart, but in the road map and in the execution of the figures. Learning how to follow the chart and orchestrate ensemble figures in a musical fashion is an ambitious goal.

So, fasten your seat belts and let's take a look at the first examples of ensemble figures and how to play them.

Setting Up One-Note Ensemble Figures

On-The-Beat Accents

When you approach an ensemble figure, two questions need to be addressed:

1. What do I play?

2. Where do I play it?

The second question is easy. The typical set-up is ON THE BEAT, just before the ensemble figure. For example, if the figure falls on beat 1, a typical set-up will fall on beat 4 of the previous bar.

The first question, what to play, is a little more involved, so let's start with the most basic set-up: the Single-Note Set-Up.

Play a single snare drum note ON THE BEAT, just before the written figure—in this case, beat 4. Then crash the written ensemble figure on beat 1, supported with the bass drum, and go back to time on the following beat.

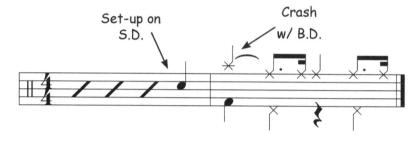

We can also invert the orchestration so the set-up is played by the bass drum (in this case, beat 4) and the ensemble figure on beat 1 is crashed and supported by the snare drum.

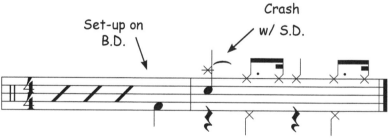

This note—the one before the crash—is often called the "send-off" note because it sends the band into the figure.

This concept of opposing sounds is very important, so remember:

1. If you play the send-off note with snare drum, crash the figure with the bass drum.

2. If you play the send-off note with bass drum, crash with the snare drum.

The stickings in this book reflect a right-handed approach; left-handed players can reverse the stickings. However, many right-handed students have asked why they shouldn't crash with the left hand. This is simply a matter of consistancy and ease of explanation. Once you feel comfortable with the techniques of chart reading, you can apply these techniques to best suit your playing. However, during this initial period of using and understanding set-ups, I think it is important to "stick" with the exercises as written.

On-The-Beat Ensemble Figures

Practice each of the following examples of ensemble figures using single-note set-ups from the previous page. Start slowly, and repeat each exercise until you are comfortable at that tempo before moving on.

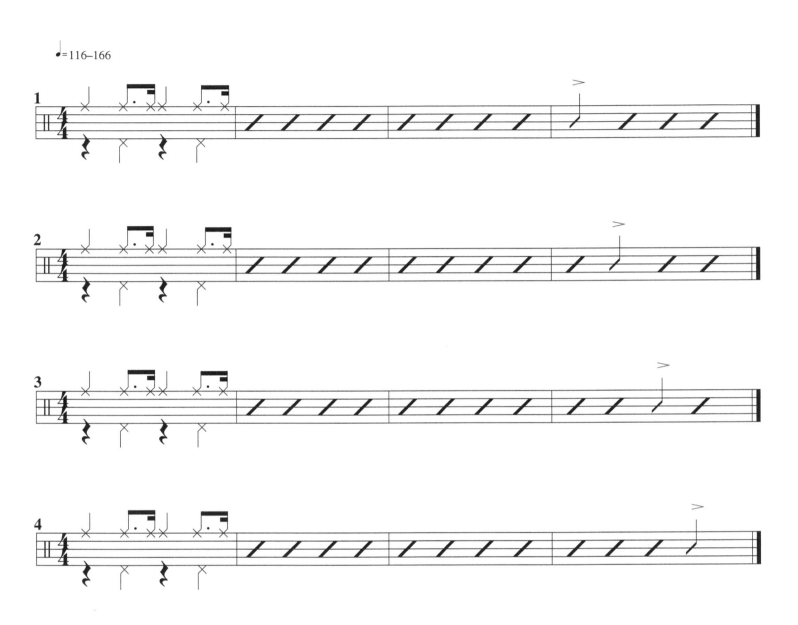

Remember, play the set-ups both ways: set-up with snare drum, accent the figure with crash cymbal and bass drum; and set-up with bass drum, accent with crash cymbal and snare drum.

Setting Up One-Note Ensemble Figures

Upbeat Accents

When the written accent falls on an upbeat, the same rules apply. For example, if the ensemble figure is on the "and" of beat 1, the set-up still falls ON THE BEAT, just before the "and"—in this example, right on beat 1.

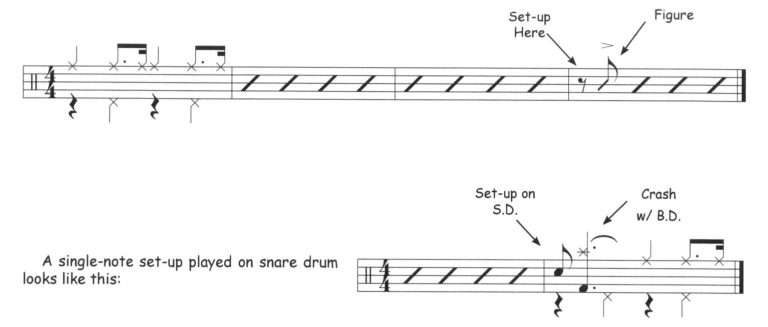

A single-note set-up played on snare drum looks like this:

Remember, if you play the set-up with snare drum, you will support the crash with bass drum.

If you invert the orchestration so the set-up is played by the bass drum (in this case, beat 1), then the ensemble figure is crashed and supported by the snare drum on the "and" of 1.

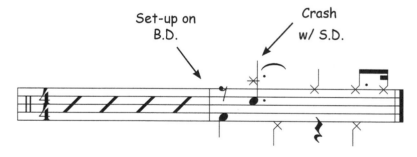

Upbeat Ensemble Figures

Practice each of the following examples of ensemble figures using set-up ideas from the previous pages.

Remember, practice your set-ups both ways: setting up with snare drum, accenting with crash cymbal and bass drum; then setting up with bass drum, accenting with crash cymbal and snare drum.

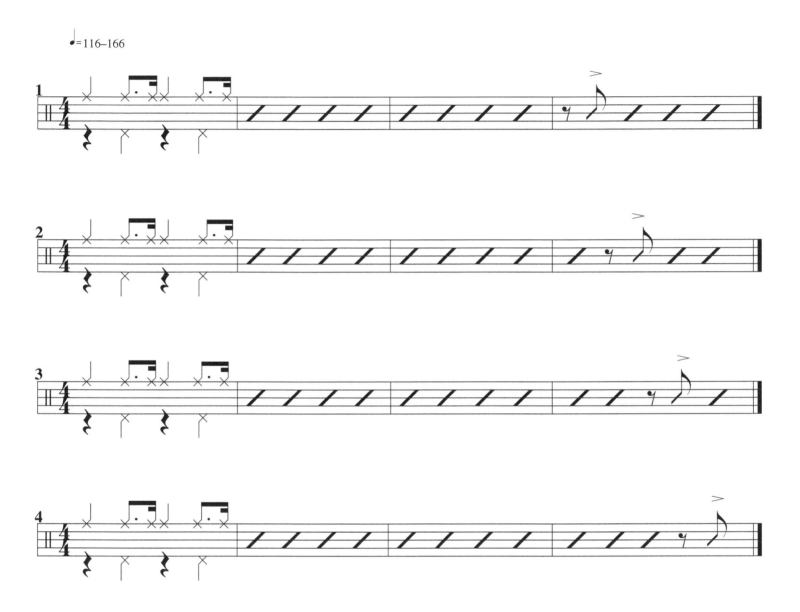

You may have noticed that a set-up played on beat 1 will work for an ensemble figure written on the "and" of 1 **or** for a figure on beat 2. A set-up played on beat 2 can be used for a figure written on the "and" of 2 **or** for a figure on beat 3, and so on.

With that in mind, there are only four basic places to play set-ups: beat 1, beat 2, beat 3 and beat 4. These four places will work as set-ups for ALL downbeats and upbeats in 4/4 time.

Embellishing The Single-Note Set-Up

Taking the single-note set-up a step further, you can embellish the set-up to further enhance the ensemble figure.

Single-Note Set-Up

Possible Orchestrations

1. Adding a grace note turns the single-note set-up into a flam and gives it more power. Experiment with sounds by moving the grace note to different toms. (Usual sticking of the flam is rL, to prepare the right hand for the impending cymbal crash.)

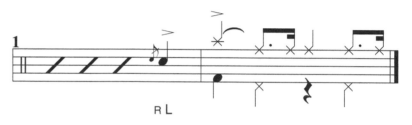

2. Adding two grace notes turns the single note into a 3-stroke ruff, further enhancing the set-up. Again, experiment with moving the grace notes onto other toms for different possibilities. (Usual sticking of the ruff is lrL, to prepare the right hand for the cymbal crash.)

2a. The inverted 3-stroke ruff, leading into a bass drum set-up on beat 4. Now the ensemble figure is accented with the crash cymbal and snare drum.

3. A swing 8th note leading into the send-off note is very typical of the big-band style. End the set-up with the left hand to facilitate a right-hand crash.

3a. A swing 8th note with an "inverted" orchestration.

4. Expanding the set-up further, play 8th-note triplets leading into the send-off note. (End the set-up with the left hand to prepare for the right-hand crash.)

RLRL

4a. The same triplet rhythm now orchestrated leading into a bass drum set-up. Remember to experiment with different orchestrations around the toms.

RLR

5. This is a variation of the 3-stroke ruff, leading with a strong punch on the send-off beat. (The sticking here ends with the left hand to prepare for the right hand crash.)

R LRL

5a. Same as above, inverted so the ensemble figure is supported with the snare drum.

R LR

6. Playing a 16th-note set-up against the swing 8th note creates a feeling of rhythmic tension that can be a very effective tool. (End the set-up with the left hand.)

RLLRL

6a. The same 16th-note rhythm as above with an "inverted" orchestration, playing the send-off note on bass drum.

LRLR

SINGLE-NOTE ENSEMBLE FIGURES W/ DRUMS
TRACK 1

To demonstrate these set-ups and embellishments, Track 1 is a version of the chart on page 17 with drums. I utilized each of the figures on pages 13 and 14 so you can hear them with music. Following is a transcription of the orchestrations and an explanation of each figure.

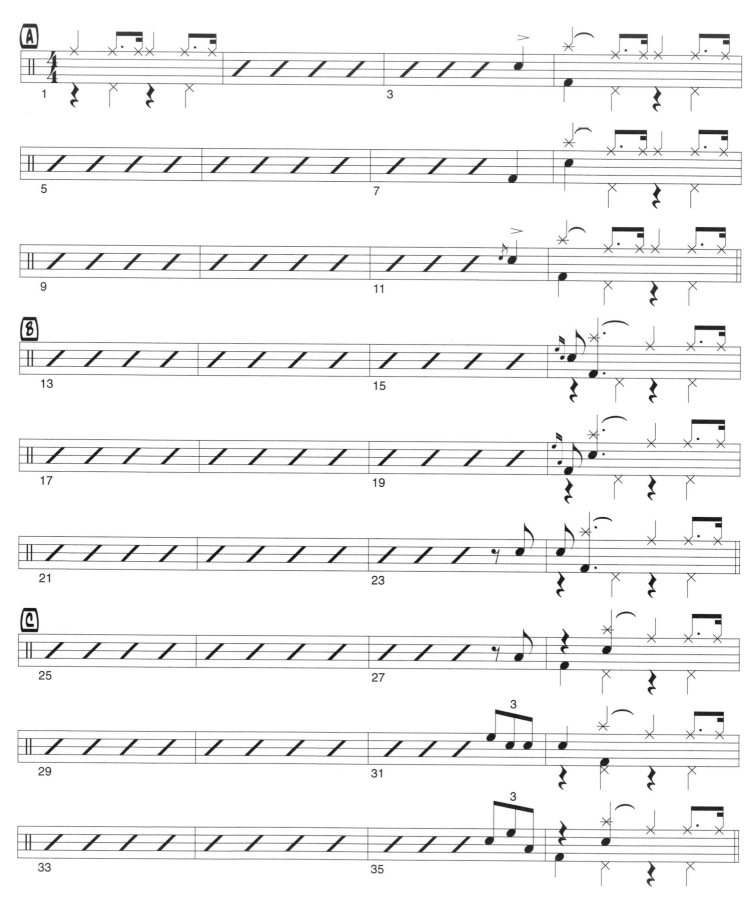

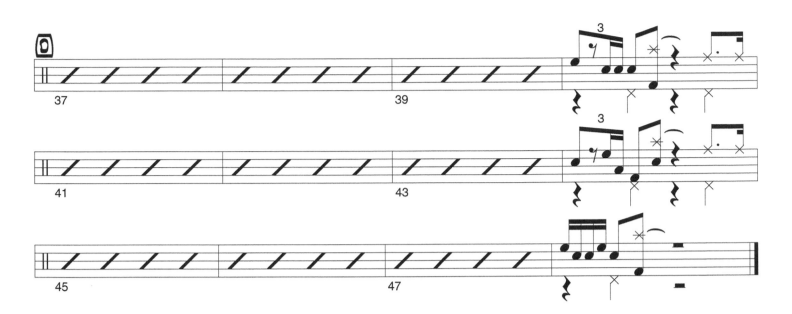

Meas. 3-4

Single-note set-up; set-up on snare drum, crash with bass drum.

Meas. 7-8

Single-note set-up; set-up on bass drum, crash with snare drum.

Meas. 11-12

Flam set-up; played on snare drum, crash with bass drum.

Meas. 16

3-stroke ruff; set-up on snare drum, crash with bass drum.

Meas. 20

3-stroke ruff; set-up on bass drum, crash with snare drum.

Meas. 23-24

Swing 8th notes; set-up on snare drum, crash with bass drum.

Meas. 27-28

Swing 8th notes; set-up on bass drum, crash with snare drum.

Meas. 31-32

8th-note triplets; end on snare drum, crash with bass drum.

Meas. 35-36

8th-note triplets; end on bass drum, crash with snare drum.

Meas. 40

Variation on the 3-stroke ruff; end on snare drum, crash with bass drum.

Meas. 44

Variation on the 3-stroke ruff; end on bass drum, crash with snare drum.

Meas. 48

16th notes; ending on snare drum, crash with bass drum.

SINGLE-NOTE ENSEMBLE FIGURES #1
TRACK ❷

Track 2 is the same music as track 1, without drums. This is the first "chart" you will play with the accompanying audio. Each play-along example has two measures count-off up front to establish the time. Most big-band charts are copied by hand; each play-along chart in this text has the hand-written look as well to help you get comfortable reading in that style,

In the following chart, repeat each line three times, using different set-ups from the previous pages. Try not to rely on any one set-up too much. Also, make use of the "inverted" set-ups, using bass drum and supporting the ensemble figure with the snare drum.

♩=136

SINGLE-NOTE ENSEMBLE FIGURES #2
TRACK 3

Repeat each line three times, using different set-ups from the previous pages. You will find that certain set-ups work better at specific tempos. Again, try not to rely on any one set-up too much.

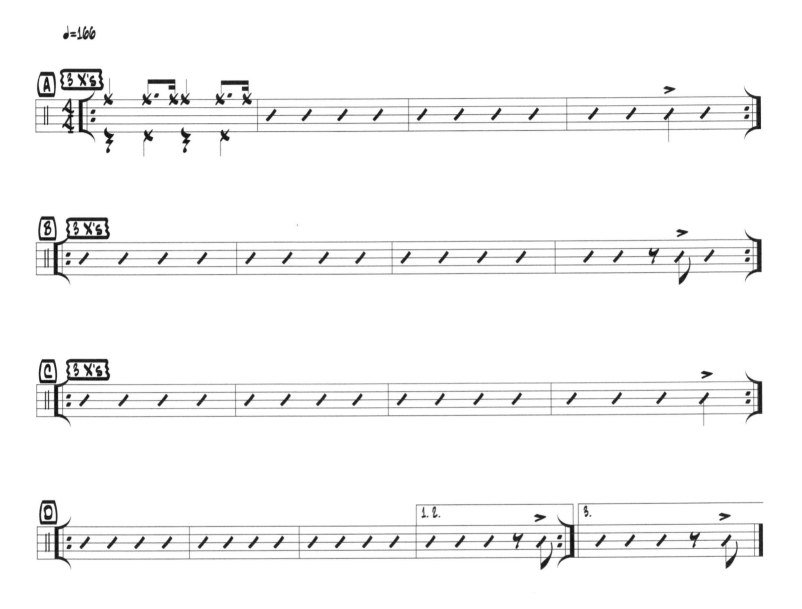

In most situations, short figures lend themselves to short set-ups; don't play a long, protracted set-up for a single 8th-note accent. (It over-emphasizes the figure.) Conversely, longer figures usually require longer set-ups. A good rule of thumb is that the set-up should be roughly as long as the figure it is meant to support. (A quarter-note accent will get approximately one beat of set-up; a dotted half-note accent should get approximately three beats of set-up, etc.)

Duration Of Notes

The duration of a written accent helps to determine its orchestration on the drums. The longer the note, the longer or more *legato* the sound should sustain. Conversely, the shorter the duration, the shorter or more *staccato* the orchestration should be. We must choose the orchestration that best suits a figure.

In the case of a longer note, we would probably use a larger, longer cymbal sound to emphasize the importance of the note. Figures with a short duration are best played on cymbals with a quick decay time.

1. In this example, the accented figure is a dotted half-note, which has a long duration. When orchestrating this note, choose a sound that sustains (e.g., large crash cymbal with bass drum, ride cymbal, etc.).

2. When the ensemble figure has a short duration—like an 8th note—choose a sound that matches that duration (e.g., splash cymbal with snare drum, bell of ride cym., closed hi-hat with bass drum, etc.).

3. Other ways of notating the duration of a note are to write expression and articulation markings above the note. The line drawn over these notes is a legato marking, indicating they should be played with a longer duration.

4. A dot means that the note is to be played staccato, or with a short duration. Both notes in this example would be played with a staccato orchestration.

5. A "cap" accent illustrates a stronger, shorter accent than a normal accent marking.

6. A slurred note (a note followed by a phrase marking as shown) has an increased duration. In this example, even though the 8th note is usually played as a "short" note, the marking after it gives it more length.

NOT TOO SCARY
w/ Drums-Trackk ◆4◆ w/o Drums-Track ◆5◆

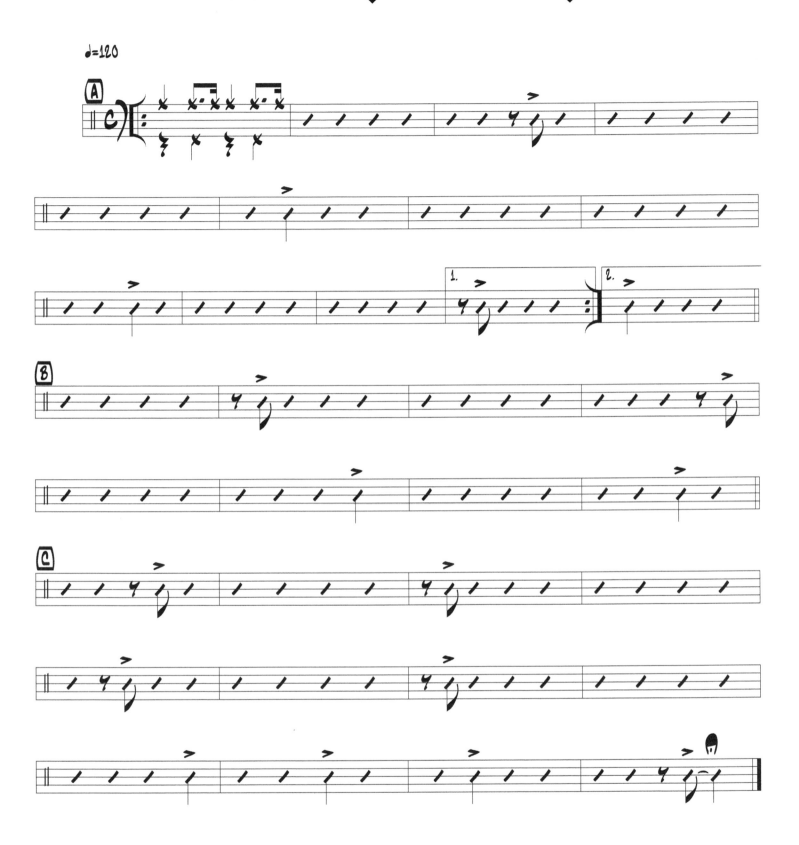

I have included a version of this chart with drums so that you can hear how these set-ups and embellishments are used in context. Do not copy the exact set-ups on the audio, instead use it to illustrate the importance of variety and color in your orchestrations of the figures.

The Road Map II

Now that you've played your first chart, let's add a few more terms to your chart-reading vocabulary. These terms are essential in following charts. As I mentioned before, a big problem in chart reading is getting lost in the "road map." Make sure you understand these items before going on.

1. D.C. or Da Capo

Indication that the piece is to be repeated from the beginning (or "top").

2. D.S. or Dal Segno

Return to the sign 𝄋 (found previously in the piece).

3. Coda

The Coda is the concluding section of the piece. It is indicated by ⊕.

4. D.C. al Coda

Return to the beginning of the piece, and play until you reach the Coda sign. At that point, jump to the Coda (marked by a matching Coda sign).

In this example, play through measures 1–8, where you would D.C. back to the beginning. At this point, play from measure 1 through the Coda sign at the end of measure 4. Then, "take the coda" by jumping to the Coda sign at the last line and play measures 13 through 14.

5. D.S. al Coda

The same as D.C. al Coda, but instead of returning to the beginning, you go back to the sign 𝄋 . Then take the Coda and play to the end of the piece.

6. ... al Fine

Fine means end; this term is most often used with a D.C. or D.S. marking. For example, when used in conjunction with a D.C. (D.C. al Fine) you return to the beginning of the piece and end at the Fine marking.

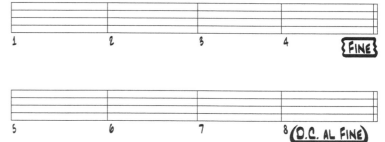

Setting Up Two-Note Ensemble Figures

Now that you're comfortable with one-note figures, the next step is learning to set up two-note ensemble figures. There are three distinct ways of handling these figures, depending on the figure itself:

- Play one set-up for both notes.
- Use one of the two notes as a set-up for the other.
- If there is enough space between the notes, use a separate set-up for each note.

Let's look at some examples of each of these possibilities.

One Set-Up For Two Accents

When there is not a lot of space between the accents, it is common to play one set-up to handle both figures, leaving the space between the figures empty. This is typical for consecutive downbeats or consecutive upbeats.

The Figure

Possible Orchestration

Since there is not a lot of space between consecutive on-the-beat quarter notes, you can play one set-up for both notes. Here, a single-stroke ruff is played on beat 4, setting up the crashes on beats 1 and 2.

The Figure

Possible Orchestration

With consecutive upbeats, there is still not enough space between the accents to set up the second 8th note. Here, a set-up before the first accent takes you from beat 4 to beat 1, and prepares the "and" of 1 as well as the "and" of 2.

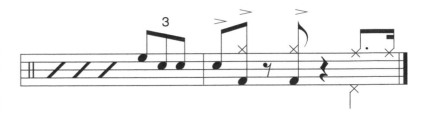

Remember, this "one set-up for two notes" principle works regardless of which beats the accents begin on, as long as they are a quarter note apart.

Using the one set-up for two notes concept, play set-ups for the following ensemble figures.

Try different orchestrations for your set-ups:

- Set-up bass drum, crash w/ snare.
- Use flams and 3-stroke ruffs.

- Set-up snare, crash w/ bass drum
- Use triplets, swing 8ths and 16th notes.

♩= 132-160

Right Next Door
Track 6

Using One Figure To Set Up The Next

In some instances, when there are two consecutive notes in an ensemble figure, the second note requires more emphasis than the first. In these cases, the first note can be used to set up the second. The importance of the notes is decided by:

- a written accent
- an implied accent
- duration

The Figure

Possible Orchestration

An implied accent is stress given to a note because of musical markings that imply its importance to the phrase. These may include dynamic markings and articulation markings (ties and slurs). Here, the slur marking on the second note implies its importance without a written accent.

. . . .

The Figure

Possible Orchestration

Duration has a lot to do with the orchestration of notes; here, the dotted half-note on beat 2 gets more emphasis than the quarter note on beat 1. In this orchestration, the 8th-note triplet leads into beat one to set up the more important figure on beat 2.

In the following exercises, use the first note to set up the longer second note.

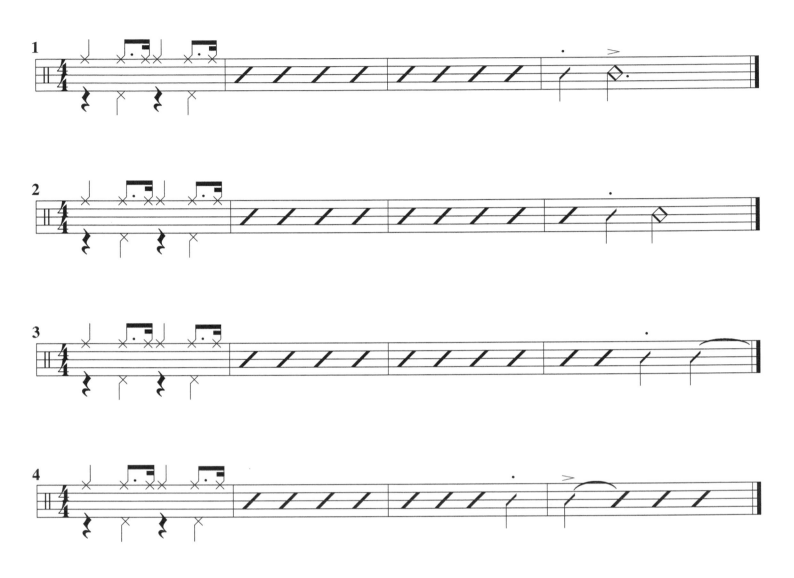

This concept of deciding which notes to set up also works with 8th notes, and is covered in a later chapter (Which Notes Are Important?).

Setting Up Each Note Separately

Starting On A Downbeat

The third possibility for two-note ensemble figures is to play a separate set-up for each note. This happens when there is more than one beat between the figures, which gives us time to play a set-up before the second accent.

As before, when the first note of a two-note ensemble figure falls on the beat, the first set-up will be played on the previous beat. In addition, we will play a second set-up before the second figure, and crash it as well. For example:

The Figure

Possible Orchestrations

A simple flam set-up played on beat 4 sets up the first accent on beat 1. The second set-up, a snare drum note on beat 2, sets up the 8th note on the "and" of 2, which is crashed and supported by bass drum.

In this example, a triplet set-up is played from beat 3 to 4, ending on bass drum. The quarter note figure on beat 1 is subsequently crashed, supported by the snare drum. A 3-stroke ruff is played to set up the "and" of 2, which is crashed with snare drum.

Setting Up Each Note Separately

Downbeat Examples

Setting Up Each Note Separately

Starting On An Upbeat

When the first note of a two-note ensemble figure falls on an upbeat, the set-up for that note falls **on** the beat, just before the figure (as before). Then we play a separate set-up for the second figure, and crash it as well. However, it is important to note that you should not start your second set-up on the beat immediately following the first figure (in this case beat 2). By leaving a small amount of space after the first figure, we give it more emphasis.

The Figure

Possible Orchestrations

Here, a flam on beat 1 sets up the accent on the "and" of 1. The second accent on beat 4 is set up by the swing 8th-note double-stops on snare and floor tom. Note the space on beat 2.

This orchestration has a 16th-note set-up beginning on beat 4, leading into the first accent. A 3-stroke ruff on beat 3 sets up the second accent on 4. Again, beat 2 is left unplayed so as not to detract from the first figure.

Setting Up Each Note Separately

Upbeat Examples

You may notice that in examples 1 and 5 there is not much space to play a set-up before the second figure. In these cases, it is acceptable to **not** play a set-up (or to play a swing 8th on the upbeat) before the second figure.

♩ = 132-160

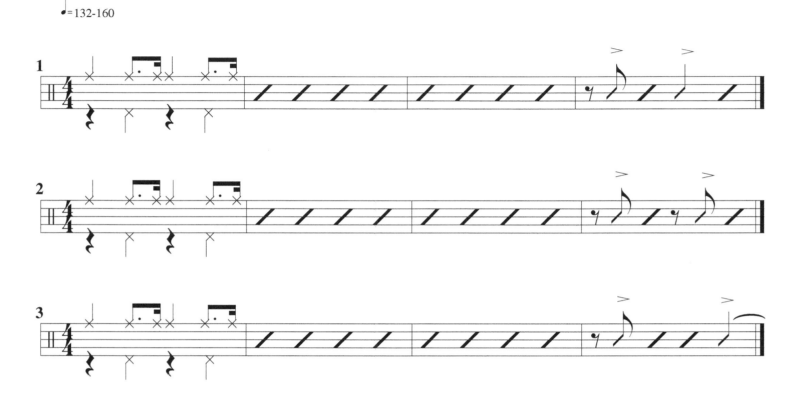

CRUISING ALONG
w/ Drums-Track ⑦   w/o Drums-Track ⑧

Monster Beneath Your Bed
Track 9

The Road Map III

Here are a few more musical terms that often appear in charts.

1. Multiple Measure Repeat Signs

Similar to the measure repeat sign, this figure means that you should repeat the indicated number of measures (most likely 2 or 4) ONCE. In this example, repeat the previous two bars one time.

2. 1st X Only

In a repeated phrase, section and ensemble figures are not always played both times through. This abbreviation tells you which time during a repeat to play the written figure. In this case, the figure is played the first time only.

3. Tacet

Don't play. This notation is often followed by a specific number, as in Tacet 16 bars or Tacet 1st X. Note the thick black line surrounding the number of measures; it could also be written as a number above a whole-note rest.

4. Vamp (or Vamp til Cue)

Repeat a section or phrase until the conductor signals the band to go on to the next section. (That signal is called a cue.)

5. Open (or Open For Solos)

"Open" is a term applied to a repeated section **during a solo**, where the band will repeat the phrase indefinitely until the soloist (or the conductor) signals the band to go onto the next section. Here, you would repeat four measures of time until the solo(s) are finished.

A Little Tougher
Track 10

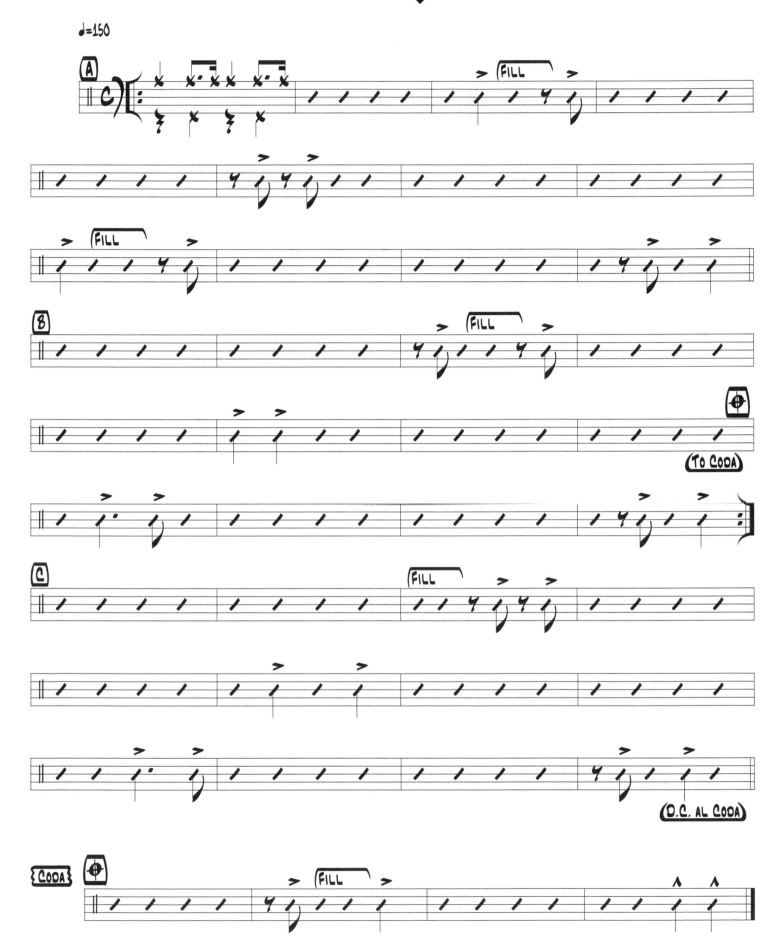

Ensemble Figures In ³/₄ Time

Now that you have an understanding of basic ensemble figures in ⁴/₄ time, the next section applies these concepts to ³/₄ . It begins with single-note ensemble figures against a ³/₄ swing pattern, then moves on to two-note figures.

³/₄ time is a common meter for big band as well as jazz and other styles of music. There are three beats in each measure, and the quarter note gets the beat.

Approach the figures the same way you would in ⁴/₄ time. Once you feel comfortable with the single accents, move on to the two-note figures.

Notice that in ³/₄ time there are six counts as a pick-up instead of eight. It is typical to have two measures of count-off leading into any song; in this case, that equals six counts.

The biggest challenge in this chapter is keeping a solid three feel while hitting the figures. Keep counting in your head; it will get easier, and ultimately you will feel the three beats without having to rely on counting.

"Whaddya mean, use more dynamics? I'm playing as loud as I can!"

Single-Note Ensemble Figures In ¾ Time
Track 11

♩=120

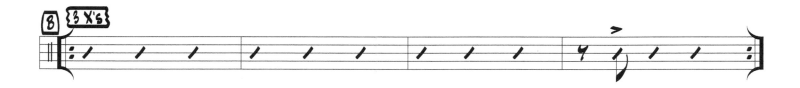

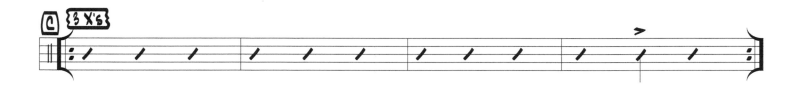

Piece Of Cake
Track 12

Two-Note Ensemble Figures In ³/₄ Time

One Set-Up Examples

As in ⁴/₄ , when two accents fall close together, it is common to play one set-up to handle both figures, leaving the space between the figures empty. Practice these examples of two-note figures in ³/₄ time.

♩=132-160

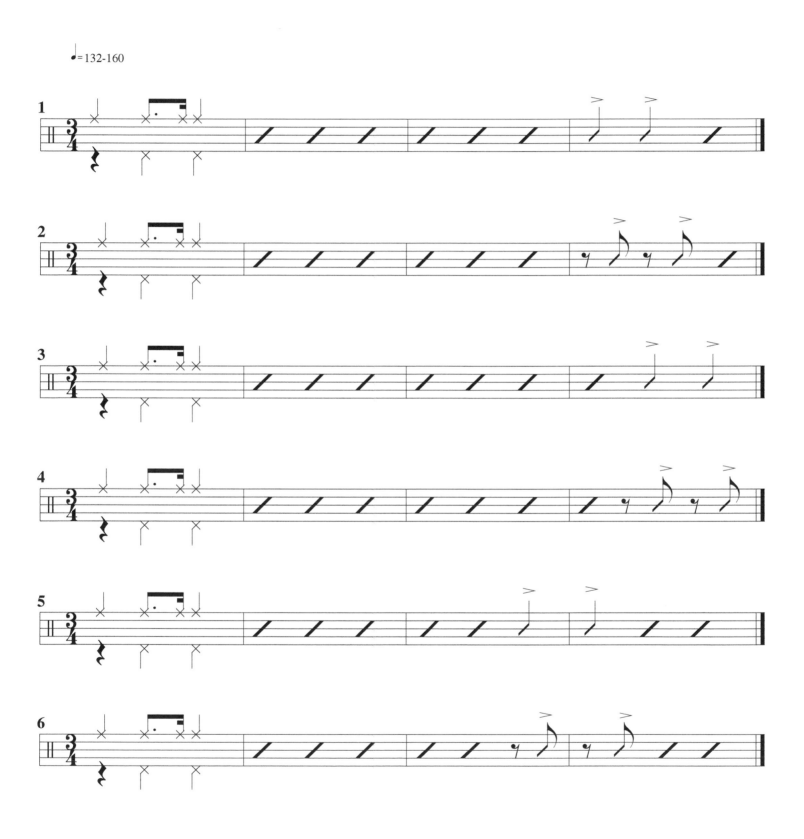

Two-Note Ensemble Figures In ³/₄ Time

Separate Set-Up Examples

Using the same concepts you learned in previous exercises, practice these examples of two-note figures using separate set-ups for each accent.

♩=132-160

Two-Note Ensemble Figures In ³/₄ Time
Track 13

♩=132

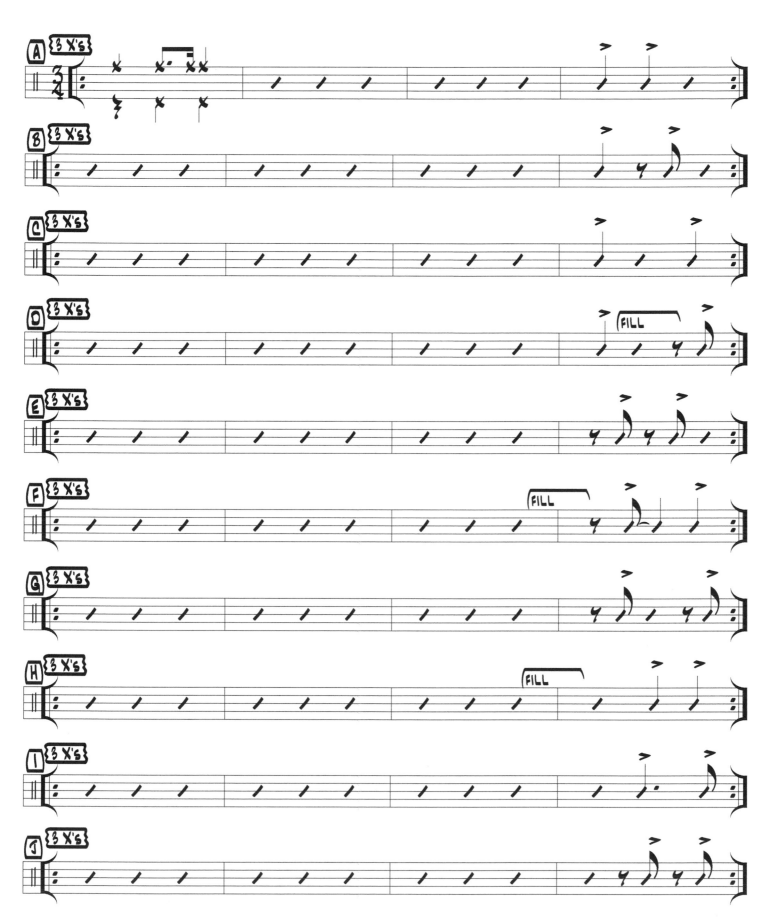

To Three, Or Not To Three
Track 14

Three-Note Ensemble Figures

One Set-Up Examples

Expanding on the concepts provided in the two-note ensemble figures, we can now create cohesive, musical set-ups for three-note ensemble figures. I have broken this into two parts; the first consists of figures next to each other, the second is combinations of accents spread across the measure.

The first group of figures is similar to the two-note figures placed next to each other. Use one set-up to handle all three figures.

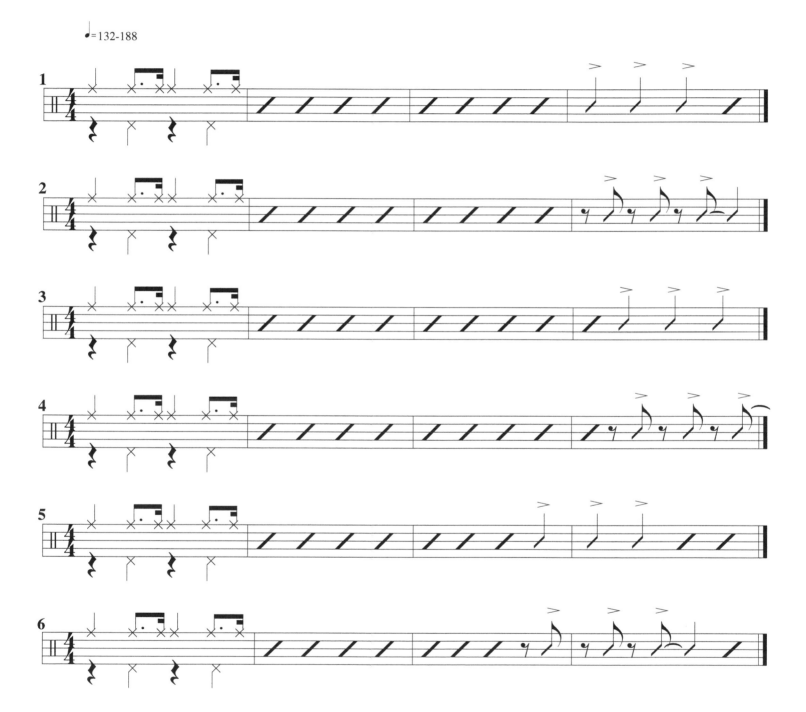

Three-Note Ensemble Figures

Multiple Set-Ups

In the next examples, the ensemble figures are spread across the measure and will require multiple set-ups. The key is to decide where to put the set-ups; remember, not every note will get one. The more you practice these, the more comfortable you will become with creating musical set-ups.

By listening to big band and jazz recordings you will hear the way other drummers support these figures and begin to assimilate those ideas into your playing.

Two Left Feet
Track ⑮

♩=152

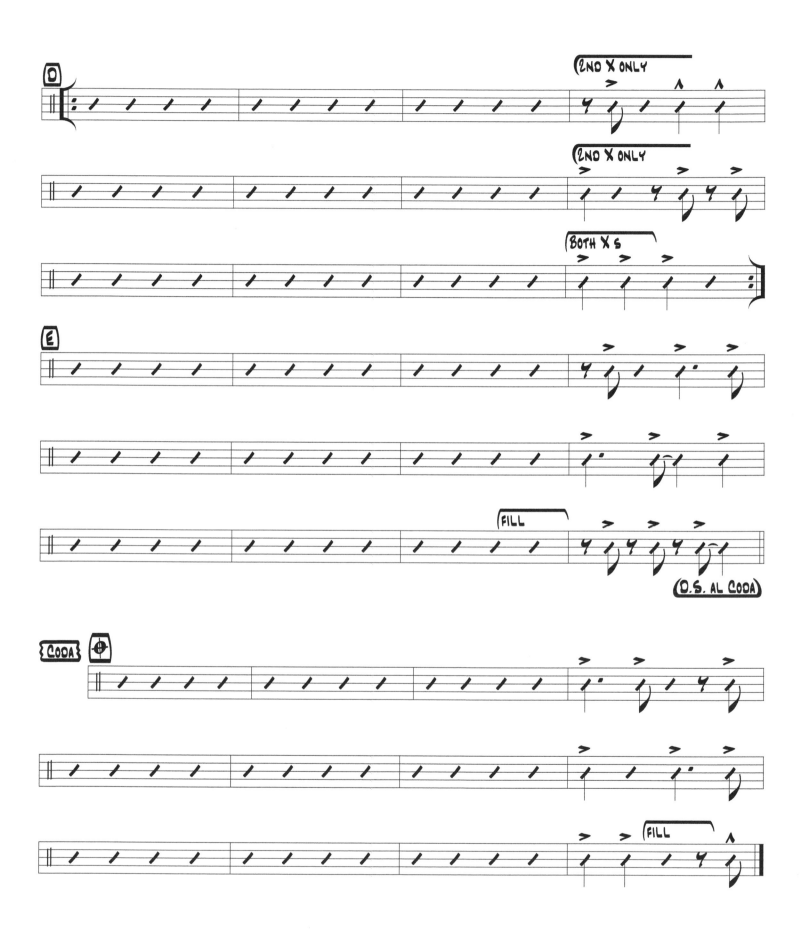

Which Notes Are Important?

Up to this point, we have dealt with simple ensemble figures, where every note has been important. However, when reading more intricate phrases, not all notes are given the same importance; indeed, certain notes in each phrase need to stand out. If all notes were played equally, ensemble phrases would be drowned out by drummers bashing every note on cymbals.

To avoid that, there are rules we can use to identify which notes are important in these situations.

Rule #1

Any note larger than an 8th note is important.

This means we can crash quarter notes, dotted-quarter notes, half notes, etc., anything larger in value than an 8th note. This also includes an 8th note tied to another note, since its value is greater than an 8th note.

Possible Orchestrations

By playing two swung 8th notes on snare drum, we can set up the more important notes that follow—in this case, the quarter note and the dotted quarter.

In this example, a flam is played on beat 1 followed by two 8th notes, with the crashes on the "and" of beats 2 and 3 supported by the bass drum.

In this case, a triplet set-up beginning on beat 1 takes us to beat 2 on bass drum. The upbeats are both crashed, supported by snare drum.

IMPORTANT: Even though some notes may be more important than others, every note written in an ensemble figure should be played.

Since anything larger than an 8th note is important, the notes requiring the most editing are the 8th notes themselves. This brings us to Rule #2.

Rule #2

An 8th note immediately followed by ANY note (including another 8th note) is NOT accented.

In this phrase, the 8th note is immediately followed by a dotted quarter. The dotted quarter, being larger than an 8th note, is accented (in other words, crashed). The 8th note is not important enough to be crashed, but still needs to be played. This technique uses "unaccented" notes to set up more important notes—in this case, the dotted quarter.

Possible Orchestrations

In this example, the first 8th note is flammed on snare drum and used to set up the dotted-quarter note, which is crashed on the "and" of 1.

Here we start our set-up on the beat before the figure begins (in this case, swung 8th notes starting on beat 4). This gives the set-up more length and power.

This is the same idea as above, but uses a 16th-note variation ending on beat 1 in the bass drum. The dotted quarter is then crashed, supported by the snare drum.

IMPORTANT: Even though some notes may be more important than others, every note written in an ensemble figure should be played. Later, if you choose to leave certain notes out of a figure, it will be for musical reasons, not technical ones.

All that remains now are 8th notes followed by rests. This brings us to Rule #3.

Rule #3

An 8th note immediately followed by any rest is important.

    In this example, the first 8th note of each group is immediately followed by other 8th notes. The third 8th note is followed by a rest. Therefore, the third 8th note is the important one, and is accented with a crash. (Notes followed by time slashes are also interpreted as important.)

Possible Orchestrations

The first two 8th notes are played on snare drum and are used to set up the last 8th note, which is crashed, supported by the bass drum. Notice the space following the accent on the "and" of 2.

For a longer set-up, we can start before the figure itself. Here, we begin on beat 4 with 8th-note triplets leading into beat 1, playing the "and" of 1 and beat 2 and crashing on the "and" of 2.

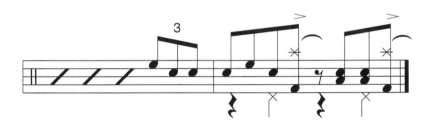

In this example, 16th notes are used to set up the figure, ending with bass drum on beat 4, and crashing the "and" of 2 supported by the snare drum.

    IMPORTANT: Even though some notes may be more important than others, every note written in an ensemble figure should be played. Later, if you choose to leave certain notes out of a figure, it will be for musical reasons, not technical ones.

What's Important?

Examples #1

Each of these measures is a typical syncopated ensemble figure. Using the rules on the previous pages, write accents over the important notes; then come up with possible orchestrations for each example. Remember to use the unaccented notes to help set up the more important accents.

Which Notes Are Important? (cont.)

Rule #4 deals with a very specific figure found in many big band ensemble phrases.

Rule #4

Four 8th notes beamed together: accent first and last notes.

In this example, the first 8th note on beat 1 is accented, the "and" of 1 and beat 2 are played, and the "and" of beat 2 is accented. (Remember to swing the 8th notes.)

Possible Orchestrations

The first 8th note is accented with a crash, and the middle two 8th notes are played on snare drum. The last 8th note on the "and" of 2 is crashed, supported by the bass drum.

Using a simple set-up, we can start before the figure itself; here, we begin with a flam on beat 4 leading into the figure on beat 1.

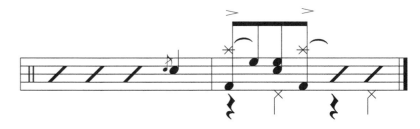

In this example, a triplet set-up is played from beat 3 to 4, ending on bass drum. The 8th note on beat 1 is subsequently crashed, supported by the snare drum. The middle notes of the figure are then played, with the 8th note on the "and" of 2 being crashed.

Rule #5 is a specific case that contradicts Rule #1.

Rule #5

Consecutive on-the-beat quarter notes may be played, not crashed.

In this example, quarter-note accents fall on each beat in the measure; however, crashing each one of these quarter notes will probably drown out whatever the band is playing. Thus, whenever we have consecutive on-the-beat accents, we may play them without crashes.

Possible Orchestrations

Each of the quarter notes may be interpreted as the same sound; in this case, all notes are played on snare drum.

Example B uses a drag on beat 4 to set up the figure. On beats 1 and 2, the first two notes of the ensemble figure are played with the bass drum; the last two, on beats 3 and 4, are played on snare drum.

In this example, a triplet set-up is played from beat 3 to 4, ending on bass drum. The first quarter-note ensemble figure is played on snare drum, alternating the subsequent quarter notes between bass and snare.

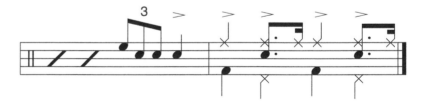

What's Important?

Examples #2

Each of these measure is a typical syncopated ensemble figure. Using the rules on the previous pages, write accents over the important notes; then come up with possible orchestrations for each example. Remember to use the unaccented notes to help set up the more important accents.

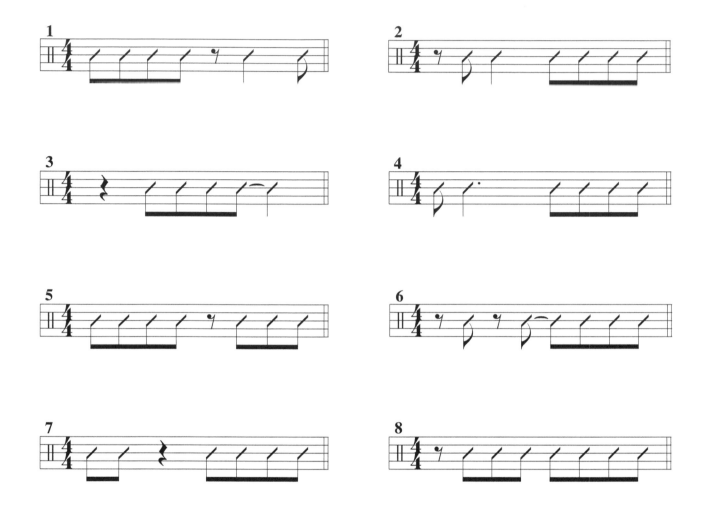

The Musical Question

Now that you have developed the technique to play a variety of ensemble figures, perhaps the most important concept is when NOT to play a figure. Don't feel that you must play every figure, especially at the expense of timekeeping. First and foremost, our job as drummers is to establish and maintain the time. Many students get so involved hitting the figures that the groove goes out the window.

Once you have the developed the ability to set up figures comfortably, deciding which ones to set up becomes a musical question. This question can only be answered by experience, both playing and listening. You must use your ears and your musical experience to take the techniques you have learned in this text and apply them to best suit each musical situation you encounter.

The Biggest Wagon
Track ⟨16⟩

MUSICIANS INSTITUTE PRESS is the official series of Southern California's renowned music school, Musicians Institute. MI instructors, some of the finest musicians in the world, share their vast knowledge and experience with you – no matter what your current level. For guitar, bass, drums, vocals, and keyboards, MI Press offers the finest music curriculum for higher learning through a variety of series:

ESSENTIAL CONCEPTS
Designed from MI core curriculum programs.

MASTER CLASS
Designed from MI elective courses.

PRIVATE LESSONS
Tackle a variety of topics "one-on one" with MI faculty instructors.

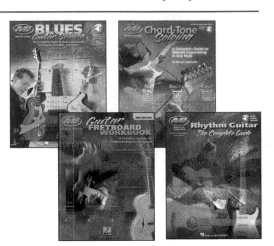

GUITAR

Acoustic Artistry
by Evan Hirschelman • Private Lessons
00695922 Book/Online Audio $19.99

Advanced Scale Concepts & Licks for Guitar
by Jean Marc Belkadi • Private Lessons
00695298 Book/CD Pack $19.99

All-in-One Guitar Soloing Course
by Daniel Gilbert & Beth Marlis
00217709 Book/Online Media $29.99

Blues/Rock Soloing for Guitar
by Robert Calva • Private Lessons
00695680 Book/CD Pack $19.99

Blues Guitar Soloing
by Keith Wyatt • Master Class
00695132 Book/Online Audio $29.99

Blues Rhythm Guitar
by Keith Wyatt • Master Class
00695131 Book/Online Audio $19.99

Dean Brown
00696002 DVD $29.95

Chord Progressions for Guitar
by Tom Kolb • Private Lessons
00695664 Book/Online Audio $19.99

Chord Tone Soloing
by Barrett Tagliarino • Private Lessons
00695855 Book/Online Audio $24.99

Chord-Melody Guitar
by Bruce Buckingham • Private Lessons
00695646 Book/Online Audio $19.99

Classical & Fingerstyle Guitar Techniques
by David Oakes • Master Class
00695171 Book/Online Audio $19.99

Classical Themes for Electric Guitar
by Jean Marc Belkadi • Private Lessons
00695806 Book/CD Pack $15.99

Country Guitar
by Al Bonhomme • Master Class
00695661 Book/Online Audio $19.99

Diminished Scale for Guitar
by Jean Marc Belkadi • Private Lessons
00695227 Book/CD Pack $14.99

Essential Rhythm Guitar
by Steve Trovato • Private Lessons
00695181 Book/CD Pack $16.99

Exotic Scales & Licks for Electric Guitar
by Jean Marc Belkadi • Private Lessons
00695860 Book/CD Pack $16.95

Funk Guitar
by Ross Bolton • Private Lessons
00695419 Book/CD Pack $15.99

Guitar Basics
by Bruce Buckingham • Private Lessons
00695134 Book/Online Audio $17.99

Guitar Fretboard Workbook
by Barrett Tagliarino • Essential Concepts
00695712 .... $19.99

Guitar Hanon
by Peter Deneff • Private Lessons
00695321 .... $14.99

Guitar Lick•tionary
by Dave Hill • Private Lessons
00695482 Book/CD Pack $21.99

Guitar Soloing
by Dan Gilbert & Beth Marlis • Essential Concepts
00695190 Book/CD Pack $22.99

Harmonics
by Jamie Findlay • Private Lessons
00695169 Book/CD Pack $13.99

Harmony & Theory
by Keith Wyatt & Carl Schroeder • Essential Concepts
00695169 .... $22.99

Introduction to Jazz Guitar Soloing
by Joe Elliott • Master Class
00695161 Book/Online Audio $19.95

Jazz Guitar Chord System
by Scott Henderson • Private Lessons
00695291 .... $12.99

Jazz Guitar Improvisation
by Sid Jacobs • Master Class
00217711 Book/Online Media $19.99

Jazz, Rock & Funk Guitar
by Dean Brown • Private Lessons
00217690 Book/Online Media $19.99

Jazz-Rock Triad Improvising
by Jean Marc Belkadi • Private Lessons
00695361 Book/CD Pack $15.99

Latin Guitar
by Bruce Buckingham • Master Class
00695379 Book/Online Audio $17.99

Lead Sheet Bible
by Robin Randall & Janice Peterson • Private Lessons
00695130 Book/CD Pack $22.99

Liquid Legato
by Allen Hinds • Private Lessons
00696656 Book/Online Audio $16.99

Modern Jazz Concepts for Guitar
by Sid Jacobs • Master Class
00695711 Book/CD Pack $16.95

Modern Rock Rhythm Guitar
by Danny Gill • Private Lessons
00695682 Book/Online Audio $19.99

Modes for Guitar
by Tom Kolb • Private Lessons
00695555 Book/Online Audio $18.99

Music Reading for Guitar
by David Oakes • Essential Concepts
00695192 .... $19.99

The Musician's Guide to Recording Acoustic Guitar
by Dallan Beck • Master Class
00695505 Book/CD Pack $13.99

Outside Guitar Licks
by Jean Marc Belkadi • Private Lessons
00695697 Book/CD Pack $16.99

Power Plucking
by Dale Turner • Private Lesson
00695962 Book/CD Pack $19.95

Progressive Tapping Licks
by Jean Marc Belkadi • Private Lessons
00695748 Book/CD Pack $17.99

Rhythm Guitar
by Bruce Buckingham & Eric Paschal • Essential Concepts
00695188 Book $19.99
00114559 Book/Online Audio $24.99
00695909 DVD $19.95

Rhythmic Lead Guitar
by Barrett Tagliarino • Private Lessons
00110263 Book/Online Audio $19.99

Rock Lead Basics
by Nick Nolan & Danny Gill • Master Class
00695144 Book/Online Audio $18.99
00695910 DVD $19.95

Rock Lead Performance
by Nick Nolan & Danny Gill • Master Class
00695278 Book/Online Audio $17.99

Rock Lead Techniques
by Nick Nolan & Danny Gill • Master Class
00695146 Book/Online Audio $16.99

Shred Guitar
by Greg Harrison • Master Class
00695977 Book/CD Pack $19.99

Slap & Pop Technique for Guitar
by Jean Marc Bekaldi • Private Lessons
00695645 Book/CD Pack $17.99

Solo Slap Guitar
by Jude Gold • Master Class
00139556 Book/Online Video $19.99

Technique Exercises for Guitar
by Jean Marc Belkadi • Private Lessons
00695913 Book/CD Pack $15.99

Texas Blues Guitar
by Robert Calva • Private Lessons
00695340 Book/Online Audio $17.99

Ultimate Guitar Technique
by Bill LaFleur • Private Lessons
00695863 Book/Online Audio $22.99

HAL•LEONARD®
7777 W. BLUEMOUND RD. P.O. BOX 13819 MILWAUKEE, WI 53213
www.halleonard.com